CONCINNITY PUBLISHING

The ULTIMATE GUIDE to Beaches on Prince Edward Island, Canada

DISCOVER MAJESTIC BEACHES, RED ROCK CLIFFS, LONG STRETCHES OF SOFT SAND AND GRASSY DUNES

First edition

This book was professionally typeset on Reedsy.
Find out more at reedsy.com

Contents

Chapter 1

INTRODUCTION

Welcome to Prince Edward Island. Your Gateway to Coastal Wonder. Imagine a place where time slows, the salty breeze greets you like an old friend, and every turn in the road reveals another stretch of colored sand hugging the sparkling blue sea. Welcome to Prince Edward Island (PEI) - a captivating paradise for beach lovers, adventurers, and anyone who's ever dreamed of wandering a pristine shore in search of treasures, artifacts and sea glass washed up by the waves. Here, on this magical island, the beaches are more than just pretty places to sunbath, they're reliving stories written by wind, water, and time.

This book, The ULTIMATE GUIDE to Beaches on Prince Edward Island, Canada, is your all access pass to the most breathtaking, surprising, and soul soothing beach experiences this island has to offer. Whether you're planning your first visit or you're a seasoned traveler looking for hidden gems, you're in for an unforgettable journey. Together, we'll explore every nook and cranny of PEI's coastal treasures, from its most iconic sandy stretches to its secluded, otherworldly shores that feel like they are reserved just for you.

Meet Your Guides – We are devoted beachcombers, explorers, and storytellers. Our passion for Prince Edward Island's beaches began with a single walk along the shore, where a smooth shard of blue sea glass caught our eye. That small fragment of history opened a door to a world of wonder, and we've been hooked ever since. Over the years, we've wandered the island's coastline, uncovering its quirks, secrets, and breathtaking beauty. We've met local artists who turn driftwood into masterpieces, listened to tales of shipwrecks that still leave traces in the sand, and witnessed sunsets so vivid they'd make a painter's palette blush.

This book is the result of our journey. It's our mission to share these experiences with you, so you can skip the guesswork and go straight to the good stuff. We're here to be your friendly guide, offering insider tips, heartfelt stories, and practical advice for making the most of every moment you'll spend on this island's sandy shores.

~Mari and Pam, Concinnity Publishing

What's Inside this Guide? Consider this guide your treasure map, leading you to the most extraordinary beaches on PEI. Each chapter is designed to take you deeper into the island's coastal world, showing you where to go, what to do, and why it matters. Here's a sneak peek at what's ahead:

Getting There – How to make your way to PEI, whether by bridge, ferry, cruise or air. We'll cover the smoothest routes and a few adventurous ones for the curious traveler.

PEI Tourism Facts – Before you set out, you'll want to know what makes this island special, from its climate to its unique natural features. We'll also share some surprising facts that might change the way you see PEI.

The Most Scenic, Picturesque Beachscapes Across the 3 Coastal Drives
- PEI's 3 distinct coastal drives each offer something special. You'll get a behind-the-scenes look at where to find the island's most jaw dropping beaches and hidden gems. In this chapter you will also find a list of typical artifacts found on beaches on each Coastal Drive If you've ever dreamed of finding sea glass, driftwood, or relics from the past, you're in luck.

Special Features: Island Beach Culture and Festivals by Coastal Drive
- PEI's beaches come to life with music, food, and celebration. We'll introduce you to festivals and local traditions that make this island's beach culture unforgettable.

Extra: Cruise to Île de la Madeleine from Souris, PE - Looking for even more adventure? Take a cruise to this island neighbor and uncover a whole new world of beaches to explore.

Why This Guide Will Change Your PEI Experience – This isn't your ordinary travel guide. You'll get more than just a list of "places to see". This book will guide you to connection, wonder, and discovery. Imagine knowing exactly which beach to visit if you're hunting for sea glass, driftwood or other artifacts. With this guide in hand, you'll be able to participate in the island's ongoing story.

Chapter 2

Getting There By Land, Ferry, Air, Or Cruise

Getting to Prince Edward Island is an adventure in itself, and with several options available, you can choose the journey that best suits your sense of adventure and convenience. Whether you're driving, flying, on ferry or cruise, PEI is more accessible than you might think. Here's a breakdown of how you can get to the island and what to expect from each mode of transport.

By Land: The Confederation Bridge - For many travelers, the Confederation Bridge is the most iconic way to arrive on PEI. Spanning an impressive 12.9 km (8 miles), it's the world's longest bridge over ice-covered waters. As you drive across, you'll be treated to stunning views of the Northumberland Strait. The bridge connects New Brunswick to PEI and is open year-round, making it a reliable option regardless of the season. There's a toll to leave the island via the bridge, but arrival is free - a fitting welcome for your island adventure.

By Ferry: A Scenic and Relaxing Voyage - If you prefer a more leisurely approach, hop on a ferry. Northumberland Ferries operates a scenic route between Caribou, Nova Scotia, and Wood Islands, PEI. The 75-minute journey allows you to breathe in the fresh sea air, enjoy onboard amenities, and even spot seals and seabirds along the way. The ferry is a popular choice during the warmer months and offers a relaxing way to ease into the island's pace of life. Reservations are recommended, especially in the peak season.

By Air: Fast and Direct - Flying to PEI is quick and convenient. The Charlottetown Airport (YYG) welcomes direct flights from major Canadian cities like Toronto, Montreal, and Halifax, with seasonal routes from other locations. If you're coming from farther away, you can connect through larger hubs. Once you land, you're just minutes from PEI's capital city, Charlottetown, and its surrounding beachscapes. For travelers with limited time, flying is the fastest way to start your island adventure.

By Cruise: Arrive in Style - For those seeking a grand entrance, consider arriving by cruise ship. Charlottetown Harbor is a popular stop for cruise lines exploring the Atlantic provinces. While you'll have limited time on the island, you'll still get a taste of its beauty. Excursions often include visits to the island's famous beaches, lighthouses, and cultural landmarks. If you're on a cruise itinerary, be sure to make the most of your time ashore.

Choosing Your Adventure - No matter how you arrive, each option has its own charm. The bridge is iconic, the ferry is serene, the flight is fast, and the cruise is elegant. Whichever route you choose, you'll be rewarded with an unforgettable experience on the shores of Prince Edward Island.

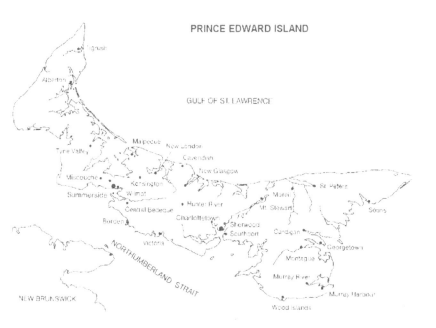

PRINCE EDWARD ISLAND

Imagine what you are about to see: Close your eyes and as you approach the island, take a moment to soak it all in. The shoreline with driftwood, red cliffs, golden beaches, and lush green pastures come into view, promising adventure, relaxation, and discovery.

Chapter 3

PEI Tourism Facts

Visitor and Information Centers - Prince Edward Island's network of Visitor Information Centers (VICs) is your first stop for local guidance. Scattered across the island's major entry points and popular destinations, these centers are packed with helpful resources, from maps and brochures to personal recommendations from friendly local staff. Whether you need directions to a hidden beach or tips on upcoming festivals, the VICs are ready to help. IMPORTANT: You can request a map of the island and a visitors' guide in advance of your arrival so that you are familiar with the routes and equipped with directions to beaches that you will find in this book. Go to https://www.tourismpei.com/visitors-guide for this information.

Getting Around the Island – Once you're on the island, getting around is a breeze. Most visitors rent a car for the freedom to explore at their own pace, but you'll also find options for bicycles, taxis, and seasonal shuttle services. PEI's scenic coastal drives are well-marked, and the island's small size means you're never far from a beach. Driving along the coast offers stunning views of red cliffs, lush green fields, and shimmering blue waters.

A Little Bit of History - PEI's story is as rich as its landscape. Originally home to the Mi'kmaq First Nation, the island's history was later shaped by Scottish, French and British settlers. The island's maritime heritage is evident in its fishing villages, lighthouses, and seafaring tales. Today, PEI's charm lies in its ability to honor the past while embracing modern tourism and beach culture. This blend of history and natural beauty creates an unforgettable experience for visitors.

An Important Note About the Ecosystem of Our Planet and on PEI (this is a direct message from Tourism PEI for readers of this book) – Residents and visitors alike love this beautiful place, and many feel a deep connection to it, as a place to play and sometimes as a place to work. The estuaries are an important resource for the shellfish industry and there are many nearshore fisheries around the Island that are linked to our coastline (Irish moss, lobster, snow crab).

The sandstone cliffs, sandy and cobble beaches and north shore dunes all form part of an extensive and ever-changing linked ecosystem. While inland mountains and prairies change slowly over geological time, we can see many changes to the Island coastline happening over the course of our lifetimes. This is a natural process, driven by winds, tides and waves. The cliffs erode and feed sand to the beaches. Woody debris and seaweed on the beaches collect sand and build dunes or coastal plains. In this way, the land in eroding cliffs is not lost, just repurposed.

The coastlines of PEI are also rich in wildlife. Many beaches, cliffs and estuaries are home to ground-nesting birds that stop at this point on the Atlantic migratory flyway to rear young every summer. Much of the coast is internationally recognized as important bird areas because of the rich habitat mix of salt marsh wetland, beach barrier ponds, sandspits and barrier islands scattered along our coast.

Our dynamic and fragile coastline faces many challenges. Sea level has been rising around the Island for 8,000 years and continues to rise at an accelerated pace now. Strong storm surges and less ice in the Gulf of St. Lawrence in recent years put pressure on shorelines and in some instances can change the shape of the shore very quickly. Our efforts to control or manage those forces often have unintended consequences. Please consider the fragility of these beautiful landscapes while you're here and walk lightly on this land.
   ~Thank you, from Tourism PEI

Chapter 4

The Most Scenic, Picturesque Beachscapes Across The 3 Coastal Drives

The 3 coastal drives on Prince Edward Island (PEI) - the North Cape Coastal Drive, Central Coastal Drive, and Points East Coastal Drive - are scenic driving routes designed to allow visitors to explore the diverse coastline of the island; essentially providing a comprehensive way to experience the island's coastal landscape by car. Here, we have identified the most majestic beaches on Prince Edward Island and included lists of common artifacts found in each area for the beachcomber in you.

North Cape Coastal Drive - Surrounding North Cape is the convening of the waters of the Gulf of St. Lawrence and the Northumberland Strait as these waterways converge over the longest natural rock reef in North America.

The Northumberland Straight features many shallow, calm beaches and the water is warm in the summer. The Gulf of St. Lawrence water tends to be cooler with more waves and wind so it is not as calm as the Straight. However, shallow regions along the Gulf are also relatively warm and calm in the summer compared to deeper open waters.

That said, because of its location in the northwestern tip of PEI, the North Cape jets out into the Gulf of St. Lawrence, making it particularly exposed to storms coming from the west or north. During a storm you may see the skies darken, swirling clouds in shades of gray, navy, and deep charcoal. Flashes of lightning may streak across the horizon, illuminating the tumultuous sea. The wind can roar with unrelenting intensity, sweeping across the open shoreline, bending grasses, twisting trees and howling through any nearby dunes or rock formations. The normally calm or gentle waves of the Gulf of St. Lawrence rise into towering, frothy whitecaps. They crash against the shoreline with thunderous force, sending spray high into the air.

Storms on PEI are, indeed a sight to be seen in all seasons. In the winter, the storms and resulting tides create miraculous natural ice formations on the coast and beyond into the freezing water. The iconic red cliffs of PEI at North Cape are dusted with snow, their vibrant color contrasting beautifully against the white of winter. The interplay of warm tones and frosty whites is a photographer's dream.

Miminegash Beach - Miminegash Beach is a serene and scenic stretch of PEI's western shore, known for its connection to the island's famous Irish Moss industry. The beach offers soft red and white sands, calm waters, and a peaceful ambiance that is perfect for beachcombing, sunbathing, and swimming. Visitors often see fishing boats harvesting Irish Moss offshore, adding a glimpse of local industry to the scenic views. The shallow, warm waters make it ideal for wading and exploring marine life in the tidal pools.

Cedar Dunes Provincial Park Beach - Cedar Dunes Provincial Park Beach is a beloved beach on the western tip of PEI, known for its iconic West Point Lighthouse, which stands as a striking silhouette against the horizon. This beach is ideal for swimming, wading, and family fun. Visitors can climb the lighthouse for panoramic views of the coastline or stroll along the long stretch of sand bordered by cedar trees. The beach has facilities like picnic areas, washrooms, and campgrounds, making it a convenient choice for a day trip or an overnight stay.

West Point Beach - West Point Beach is a picture-perfect destination known for its black-and-white striped lighthouse, red sandy beach, and gentle waves. The beach's striking natural beauty is complemented by the West Point Lighthouse Inn, where visitors can stay overnight. The sandy shores are ideal for swimming, sunbathing, and long beach walks. Its calm, shallow waters and scenic surroundings make it a favorite location for photography, especially at sunset when the sky lights up with color.

Skinners Pond Beach - Skinners Pond Beach is a quiet, uncrowded spot that offers a rugged, natural experience for visitors. It's known for its connection to the life of legendary Canadian musician Stompin' Tom Connors, whose homestead is nearby. The beach features red sand, small rock formations, and plenty of opportunities for beachcombing. The fresh sea breeze, expansive views, and local heritage add a sense of charm and nostalgia to this peaceful beach setting.

Howard's Cove Beach - Howard's Cove Beach is a small, rustic beach nestled along a quiet fishing village. The beach has a rugged coastline with red cliffs and soft sand that shift with the tides. Visitors often watch fishing boats return with fresh catches of lobster and fish, providing an authentic PEI maritime experience. This secluded spot offers a more rugged coastal adventure, with ample opportunities to explore tidal pools and beachcomb for driftwood and sea glass.

Nail Pond Beach - Nail Pond Beach is one of PEI's lesser-known, peaceful beaches that offers an untouched, natural experience. With soft sand, grassy dunes, and expansive views of the open sea, it's an ideal spot for beachgoers seeking a quiet retreat. Visitors can stroll along the secluded beach, listen to the rhythmic crash of the waves, and watch seabirds glide overhead. This hidden gem is a great spot for solitude, reflection, and discovering beach treasures like driftwood and shells.

Campbellton Beach - Campbellton Beach is a secluded, picturesque beach located on the western shore of PEI. Its serene surroundings, red sandstone cliffs, and soft sand provide a beautiful spot for walking, swimming, and relaxing. Visitors can explore the tidal pools that form at low tide, where marine life like crabs and starfish can be spotted. With its quiet atmosphere and scenic charm, Campbellton Beach offers a peaceful retreat for nature lovers and adventure seekers.

West Cape Beach - West Cape Beach is a dramatic and rugged beach known for its towering red sandstone cliffs and breathtaking views of the Gulf of St. Lawrence. This beach offers visitors the chance to experience PEI's wild, natural beauty at its finest. While swimming is limited due to the strong currents, the beach is ideal for walking along the shore, exploring caves, and beachcombing for shells and driftwood. Photographers often flock to West Cape Beach for its striking cliff formations and panoramic ocean views.

Jacques Cartier Provincial Park Beach - Named after the French explorer Jacques Cartier, this beach is part of a provincial park that offers stunning coastal scenery, family-friendly amenities, and camping opportunities. The beach features a wide stretch of soft red sand, shallow, calm waters, and scenic ocean views. It's a popular location for families with children, as it offers picnic areas, playgrounds, and washrooms. The park's camping facilities allow for an extended stay, making it a great option for multi-day beach vacations.

Kildare Capes Beach - Kildare Capes Beach is a hidden gem known for its dramatic red sandstone cliffs that rise above the sandy shore. This rugged, untouched beach is a naturalist's dream, offering incredible views of the coastline and the Gulf of St. Lawrence. Beachcombers often find unique treasures like driftwood and sea glass. The beach is less crowded than many others, providing a sense of seclusion and an opportunity to enjoy PEI's raw natural beauty.

Montrose Beach - Montrose Beach is a tranquil, family-friendly beach with shallow, calm waters and unique soft red sand. It's a perfect destination for swimming, wading, and beachcombing. The surrounding area is peaceful, with a backdrop of grassy dunes and wildflowers. Montrose Beach is a quiet escape where visitors can connect with nature and enjoy a relaxed beach experience.

Seacow Pond Beach - Seacow Pond Beach is a peaceful, rustic beach near the fishing community of Seacow Pond. The beach is a quiet retreat with views of fishing boats in the distance. The tranquil waters are suitable for wading and beachcombing. Visitors can enjoy long beach walks and explore the natural surroundings, searching for shells, driftwood, and other beach treasures.

Cape Wolfe Beach - Cape Wolfe Beach is a strikingly scenic beach known for its raw natural beauty, rugged cliffs, and dramatic views of the open sea. The beach is a peaceful spot for hiking, birdwatching, and enjoying the sounds of the crashing waves. Visitors often explore the beach's rocky outcrops and the unique coastal formations created by erosion. This beach is perfect for those looking for adventure and scenic views.

Norway Beach - Norway Beach is a secluded, quiet beach, offering visitors a chance to experience the island's pristine coastline without the crowds. This beach is ideal for long walks along the sand, beachcombing, and relaxing in the sun. The shallow waters are suitable for swimming, while the grassy dunes and cliffs offer scenic beauty for photographers and nature enthusiasts.

Tignish Shore Beach - Located near the village of Tignish, this small, charming beach offers calm waters, soft red sand, and a peaceful coastal atmosphere. The beach is family-friendly, with knee-deep waters perfect for young swimmers. Tignish Shore Beach is also known for its connection to the local fishing community, where visitors can see fishing boats and learn about PEI's maritime traditions.

Alberton Beach - Alberton Beach is a charming, family-friendly beach near the town of Alberton. It offers gentle waves, soft sand, and a calm, relaxing atmosphere. The beach is ideal for swimming, walking, and collecting seashells. The proximity to the town allows visitors to explore local shops, restaurants, and fishing heritage sites.

Cascumpec Bay Beach - Located along Cascumpec Bay, this beach offers a tranquil escape with calm, sheltered waters. The bay is ideal for kayaking, paddleboarding, and swimming. The natural beauty of the area includes coastal marshes, tidal flats, and scenic views, making it an excellent spot for birdwatching and nature walks.

Foxley River Beach - Foxley River Beach offers a quiet coastal retreat with views of the scenic Foxley River. This secluded beach is great for swimming, beachcombing, and enjoying peaceful surroundings. The calm waters make it an ideal spot for kayaking and paddleboarding.

Mill River Beach - Mill River Beach is located near the well-known Mill River Resort, offering a family-friendly beach experience. The calm sheltered waters are perfect for swimming and water sports. The nearby resort provides dining options, golf, and family activities, making it a well-rounded destination for visitors seeking a mixture of adventure and relaxation.

O'Leary Beach - O'Leary Beach is a lesser-known beach near the town of O'Leary. This beach is perfect for those looking for a quiet, peaceful retreat. Its calm waters and soft sand make it suitable for swimming, sunbathing, and beachcombing. Visitors can explore the nearby town, which is known for its ties to the island's potato farming heritage.

Common Artifacts Found on the North Cape Coastal Drive:

1. **Driftwood**: The powerful Gulf of St. Lawrence waves leave behind large, weathered driftwood pieces. These unique shapes are perfect

18

for DIY crafts or natural decor.

2. **Sea Glass**: Blue, green, and white sea glass is commonly found on beaches like Nail Pond Beach, Seacow Pond Beach, and Tignish Shore Beach.

3. **Shells**: Mussel, clam, and oyster shells are abundant, especially near harbors like Miminegash and Alberton.

4. **Fossils**: Occasionally, small fossils can be found in the sediment of the red sandstone cliffs. Marine fossils, like brachiopods, sometimes wash ashore.

5. **Red Sandstone Rocks and Pebbles**: Erosion of the iconic red sandstone cliffs leaves behind smooth red pebbles and larger rocks. These stones are often collected as natural souvenirs.

6. **Pottery Shards and Historical Artifacts**: Occasionally, old pottery pieces from shipwrecks or coastal settlements wash ashore. Broken pottery with distinct patterns or glaze can be spotted at beaches like North Cape and Skinners Pond.

7. **Shipwreck Artifacts**: Pieces of ship timber, iron nails, and wooden planks sometimes wash ashore after storms, hinting at shipwrecks in the Gulf of St. Lawrence.

8. **Fishing and Maritime Relics**: Ropes, buoys, and old fishing gear like lobster pot tags are frequently found due to the area's active fishing industry.

9. **Bottles and Coins**: Antique bottles, glass stoppers, and old coins have been found on North Cape beaches, especially after storms or high tides.

Central Coastal Drive - This coastal drive surrounds the middle section of the island. It is often referred to as "One Drive, Two Shores" because the Gulf of St Lawrence is on the north side of the island and the Northumberland Straight is directly on the south side of the island.

In this area, the Northumberland Strait is also known for its warm, calm and shallow waters. However, the calmness can vary depending on tides. Low tide often reveals extensive sandbars, where the water remains still and shallow allowing the sun to heat up its waters, especially in late summer. Here, like on the North Cape, the Gulf of St Lawrence is cooler and prone to dramatic storms. In the winter, on the Central coast, beaches transform into dramatic, windswept landscapes, with icy formations along the shore.

Cavendish Beach - Cavendish Beach is undoubtedly PEI's most famous and iconic beach, renowned for its long, sweeping shoreline of soft red and white sand framed by impressive red sandstone cliffs and lush green dunes. Part of PEI National Park, Cavendish Beach offers clear, shallow waters that are ideal for swimming, wading, and beach play. The beach is equipped with washrooms, changing rooms, and picnic areas, making it a family-friendly hotspot. Its proximity to Cavendish attractions like Green Gables Heritage Place and amusement parks makes it a must-visit for families and Anne of Green Gables fans. The natural beauty of the beach, combined with its facilities and nearby attractions, makes it one of the most popular tourist spots on the island.

Brackley Beach - Brackley Beach is a pristine stretch of golden sand framed by rolling sand dunes and surrounded by the lush natural landscape of PEI National Park. This expansive beach is ideal for swimming, sunbathing, and long walks by the shore. The calm, shallow waters make it a safe destination for families with young children. Brackley Beach offers ample parking, washrooms, and lifeguard supervision in the summer months. The beach is also a great spot for wildlife enthusiasts, with opportunities to spot seabirds, crabs, and other marine life along the shore.

Stanhope Beach - Stanhope Beach is a picturesque beach located within PEI National Park, known for its golden sands and calm, shallow waters. Visitors are treated to beautiful views of the Gulf of St. Lawrence, while the gentle waves provide ideal conditions for swimming and wading. This family-friendly beach offers washrooms, parking, and a scenic boardwalk that leads through lush sand dunes. The area is also popular for walking, beachcombing, and birdwatching, making it a peaceful destination for those looking for a more relaxed beach experience.

Cousins Shore Beach - Cousins Shore Beach is a hidden gem that offers stunning views of PEI's iconic red cliffs and the turquoise waters of the Gulf of St. Lawrence. This quiet, lesser-known beach provides a more secluded experience for visitors seeking tranquility. The soft sand and shallow waters make it a family-friendly spot for swimming, wading, and picnicking. Cousins Shore is also a popular beachcombing destination, where visitors can search for shells, driftwood, and sea glass.

Darnley Basin Beach - Darnley Basin Beach offers a peaceful and quiet setting for beachgoers looking for a natural escape. Surrounded by rolling dunes and salt marshes, it's an ideal place for kayaking, paddleboarding, and exploring tidal pools. The beach's balmy waters are perfect for swimming and water activities. It's quiet, natural ambiance makes it a great destination for birdwatchers, photographers, and anyone seeking a slower-paced beach experience.

Thunder Cove Beach - Thunder Cove Beach is one of the most photographed beaches on PEI, known for its iconic red sandstone formations, including the famous "Tea Cup Rock." This secluded beach is surrounded by striking red cliffs, creating a dramatic coastal landscape. The soft white sands, calm waters, and unique rock formations make Thunder

Cove a prime spot for photography, beach walks, and exploring sea caves. It's a must-visit location for those looking for Instagram-worthy views and natural beauty.

Malpeque Beach - Located near the world-famous Malpeque Oyster Bay, Malpeque Beach is a peaceful retreat for beachgoers. The beach offers soft white sand, calm waters, and a tranquil setting perfect for swimming, beachcombing, and relaxing walks. With its connection to the local oyster industry, visitors can experience the freshest seafood at nearby restaurants. Malpeque Beach is a hidden gem for those looking for a quiet, scenic beach away from the more crowded tourist areas.

Cabot Beach Provincial Park - Cabot Beach is the largest park in Western PEI and a top destination for families and campers. The wide sandy beach, calm shallow waters, and lifeguard supervision in the summer make it a safe, family-friendly location for swimming and beach activities. The park also features campgrounds, playgrounds, picnic areas, and stunning views of Malpeque Bay. Visitors can enjoy kayaking, paddleboarding, and fishing in the sheltered bay, or take a stroll along the scenic trails within the park.

Twin Shores Beach - Twin Shores Beach is part of a popular beachfront campground that offers fun and excitement for the whole family. This beach features a blend of natural beauty and resort-like amenities. Its calm, shallow waters are ideal for swimming, kayaking, and paddleboarding. Campers can enjoy direct access to the beach, while facilities like playgrounds, canteens, and on-site activities create a lively atmosphere.

Belmont Provincial Park Beach - Located along the shores of Malpeque Bay, Belmont Provincial Park Beach is a quiet beach with warm, shallow waters. The park offers picnic facilities, walking trails, and playgrounds, making it a popular spot for families and outdoor enthusiasts. Visitors can also explore the scenic boardwalk, which offers panoramic views of Malpeque Bay.

Chelton Beach Provincial Park – Chelton Beach is a charming beach with red sands, scenic views of the Confederation Bridge, and calm, warm waters. Its shallow, sandy shores make it a safe and family-friendly location for swimming, beach games, and building sandcastles. The park features picnic areas, playgrounds, and parking, offering everything needed for a fun beach day.

Seaview Beach – Seaview Beach is a quiet, unspoiled beach that provides visitors with a peaceful coastal escape. The beach's natural beauty, with its red cliffs and soft white sand, creates a scenic setting for swimming, walking, and beachcombing. This uncrowded spot offers a more private, secluded beach experience.

New London Bay Beach – New London Bay Beach is a scenic beach framed by grassy sand dunes and calm waters. It's a fantastic spot for kayaking, paddleboarding, and fishing. It's quiet, natural setting offers stunning views of the water, while the surrounding bay is home to a variety of marine life and seabirds.

North Rustico Beach – North Rustico Beach offers a blend of small-town charm and scenic beauty. Visitors can watch fishing boats come and go from the harbor, enjoy fresh seafood at local restaurants, and relax on the sandy beach. The area is ideal for swimming, kayaking, and walking along the coast.

Tracadie Beach – Tracadie Beach is known for its expansive shoreline and secluded atmosphere. Located near Tracadie Bay, the beach features white sand, calm waters, and soft dunes. It's a peaceful location for walking, beachcombing, and birdwatching.

Blooming Point Beach - Blooming Point Beach is a long, secluded beach with soft golden sand and rolling dunes. It's a local favorite for quiet walks, swimming, and beachcombing. With minimal development, Blooming Point provides a peaceful, natural environment where visitors can enjoy the beauty of PEI's coastline.

Argyle Shore Provincial Park Beach - This scenic beach is located along the South Shore and is known for its red sand and sandstone cliffs. Visitors can explore tide pools filled with marine life like crabs and periwinkles. The park features picnic facilities, scenic lookouts, and a playground.

Canoe Cove Beach - Canoe Cove Beach offers red sands, sandstone cliffs, and gentle tidal pools where kids can explore. The beach is ideal for swimming, sunbathing, and relaxing with family. Canoe Cove is a local favorite for its calm, friendly atmosphere.

Victoria Provincial Park Beach - Victoria Provincial Park Beach offers sandy shores, playgrounds, and scenic views of Victoria-by-the-Sea. The park is ideal for picnicking, walking, and beach activities. Its location near the village of Victoria gives visitors access to quaint shops, restaurants, and artisan boutiques.

Common Artifacts Found on the Central Coastal Drive:

1. **Driftwood**: Since Central Coastal beaches are more open and exposed to the elements, driftwood is often found scattered along

the shore. Beaches like Rustico and Cousins Shore are great for finding large, sculptural pieces.

2. **Sea Glass**: Sea glass is less common at groomed beaches like Cavendish, but Cousins Shore, Seaview Beach, and New London Bay Beach are great places to search.

3. **Shells**: Sand dollars, clams, and oyster shells are frequently found along Brackley and Stanhope Beaches. Walking the shoreline after a storm is the best time to find intact sand dollars.

4. **Fossils**: Central Coastal Drive is not known for fossils, but small marine fossils may be spotted in weathered rocks or cliffs.

5. **Red Sandstone Rocks and Pebbles**: The red sandstone cliffs erode into smooth red pebbles, which are common along Cavendish Beach and Thunder Cove Beach. Some are collected and polished by local artisans to create jewelry or keepsakes.

6. **Pottery Shards and Historical Artifacts**: Pottery shards may be found near the edges of small fishing communities, like North Rustico Beach, especially after coastal erosion.

7. **Shipwreck Artifacts**: While less common than in the Points East and North Cape regions, strong storms can sometimes unearth shipwreck debris.

8. **Fishing and Maritime Relics**: Lobster pot tags, old buoys, rope, and fragments of fishing gear are frequently found along Rustico and Darnley Basin Beaches. These relics reflect the long history of fishing in the area.

9. **Bottles and Coins**: Storms occasionally unearth old bottles, stoppers, and coins from the sand. Tourists sometimes spot these after storms or tidal changes at Rustico Beach, Seaview Beach, and Twin Shores Beach.

Points East Coastal Drive – The Gulf of St. Lawrence is to the north of PEI, this body of water is part of the Atlantic Ocean. The Northumberland Strait is located to the south of PEI, this body of water is separated from the Canadian mainland by PEI. These waters surround Points East Coastal Drive.

On the Northumberland Strait side, the waters are generally calmer due to protection from the Strait's shallowness and sheltering landforms. Here, water temperatures tend to be some of the warmest in PEI. The Strait's shallow depths allow the sun to warm the water quickly during summer months. On the Gulf side, the waters can be rougher, especially in exposed areas or during storms and windy weather. The water tends to be cooler than the Strait, though shallow areas can warm up significantly during sunny summer days. Winter shorelines in this area take on a surreal, ice carved beauty, resembling miniature seascapes of glistening icebergs.

Basin Head Beach - Basin Head Beach is one of PEI's most iconic and beloved beaches, famous for its "singing sands" that produce a unique squeaking sound when walked upon. The beach features powdery white sand, warm shallow waters, and a lagoon-like area known as "the run," where daring visitors can leap off a bridge into the gentle current. Basin Head is part of a larger day-use park complete with washroom facilities, changing areas, a canteen, and a museum dedicated to local fisheries history. Its family-friendly atmosphere, combined with its soft sands and calm swimming conditions, makes it a must-visit destination for beachgoers of all ages.

Red Point Beach - Red Point Beach is a scenic and secluded haven that offers visitors a mix of soft white sands and dramatic red sandstone cliffs. Tucked within Red Point Provincial Park, this beach is ideal for camping enthusiasts, with RV campsites located just steps from the beach. Its shallow waters make it a safe spot for swimming, and its stunning sunsets create unforgettable views. Beachcombers often find sea glass and small shells along the shore, while the proximity to the camping area makes it a perfect beach for an overnight seaside adventure.

Souris Beach - Located near the charming town of Souris, Souris Beach is a quiet, family-friendly beach with calm, shallow waters perfect for wading, swimming, and playing. Its boardwalk offers an easy stroll with picturesque views of fishing boats bobbing in the harbor. Souris Beach is also a popular launch point for ferry travelers heading to the Île's de la Madeleine. The beach's shore is known for small tidal pools that delight children searching for crabs, snails, and seaweed, making it a great spot for nature exploration.

Panmure Island Beach - Panmure Island Beach is one of PEI's most scenic coastal gems, known for its long, curving stretch of white sand and breathtaking ocean views. Accessed via a narrow causeway, this beach is part of Panmure Island Provincial Park, which offers picnic areas, washrooms, and parking. The beach is a fantastic spot for swimming, sunbathing, and seashell hunting. The nearby Panmure Island Lighthouse, the oldest wooden lighthouse on the island, adds to the beach's historic charm, providing visitors with an iconic photo backdrop.

Greenwich Beach - Part of Prince Edward Island National Park, Greenwich Beach is a hidden treasure celebrated for its striking sand dunes and floating boardwalk that meanders over tranquil wetlands. The beach is a naturalist's paradise, where visitors can walk the boardwalk trail before arriving at a serene, expansive shoreline with powdery sand and crystal-clear waters. As a protected area, Greenwich Beach offers a pristine, untouched atmosphere, making it a haven for photographers, hikers, and those seeking a peaceful connection with nature.

North Lake Beach - Known as the "Tuna Capital of the World," North Lake Beach is a lesser-known spot but a peaceful retreat for visitors. The beach features golden sands and is flanked by the calm, shallow waters of North Lake. It's a great spot for beachcombing, swimming, and simply relaxing in nature. The nearby harbor is a hub for deep-sea fishing excursions, and visitors can watch fishing boats return with their catch of the day.

Bothwell Beach - Bothwell Beach is a secluded stretch of unspoiled shoreline, offering tranquility and solitude for beachgoers looking for a quiet escape. Surrounded by grassy dunes, this beach is a natural retreat for sunbathers, swimmers, and beachcombers. With few crowds, it provides a peaceful experience where visitors can listen to the gentle crash of waves and spot seabirds soaring overhead. Beachcombing at Bothwell often yields treasures like driftwood, shells, and sea glass.

Savage Harbor Beach - Savage Harbor Beach is a peaceful, scenic beach known for its calm, shallow waters and panoramic views of the horizon. Ideal for families, the beach offers soft sand and gentle waves, making it safe for young swimmers. The harbor itself is a picturesque fishing village where visitors can watch fishing boats and enjoy a taste of PEI's fresh seafood. It's a great place for sunset walks, photography, and peaceful reflection.

Naufrage Beach - Naufrage Beach, meaning "shipwreck" in French, offers a rugged coastal experience with an air of maritime mystery. The beach features natural red sandstone cliffs and a mix of sand and rocky outcrops, creating a wild, dramatic setting. This area is less commercialized, giving visitors a sense of adventure and discovery as they wander along the shoreline. The nearby Naufrage fishing village and small harbor add a local flavor, offering the chance to see working fishing boats in action.

Fortune Beach - Fortune Beach is a wide, sandy beach known for its peaceful ambiance and scenic ocean views. Located near the Fortune River, this beach offers shallow, calm waters ideal for swimming, paddleboarding, and kayaking. Beachgoers can enjoy long, leisurely strolls on the wide shoreline, and nature enthusiasts may spot seabirds and marine life in the area. Fortune Beach provides an ideal setting for a calm, rejuvenating day by the sea.

St. Peters Harbor Beach - St. Peters Harbor Beach is a serene, hidden gem with golden sands, gentle waves, and a backdrop of lush sand dunes. The beach is accessible by foot along a picturesque path, adding to its feeling of seclusion and exclusivity. It's a peaceful spot for swimming, sunbathing, and walking along the pristine shoreline. Visitors can also spot remnants of an old lighthouse, offering a nostalgic reminder of the island's maritime past.

Lakeside Beach - Lakeside Beach is a long, sweeping beach known for its soft, white sand and shallow waters that are perfect for family fun. With easy access and ample parking, it's a convenient beach for visitors of all ages. This beach offers beautiful views of the Gulf of St. Lawrence and is a favorite for sunbathing, sandcastle building, and taking leisurely walks along the shore.

Kingfisher Beach - Kingfisher Beach is a quiet, natural beach with minimal development, offering visitors an escape into pure island beauty. Its calm, shallow waters make it a great spot for swimming, wading, and kayaking. Surrounded by natural greenery and grassy dunes, Kingfisher Beach feels like a hidden retreat where visitors can relax, watch for seabirds, and collect unique beach artifacts like shells and driftwood.

Campbell's Cove Beach - Campbell's Cove Beach is a scenic, rustic beach where tranquility and natural beauty take center stage. Visitors are drawn to its dramatic views of rugged cliffs, red sandstone formations, and the Gulf of St. Lawrence. With campgrounds nearby, it's a popular spot for overnight stays, offering the chance to wake up to the sound of waves crashing on the shore. The beach is ideal for swimming, fishing, and exploring natural tidal pools.

Sally's Beach - Nestled in a picturesque cove, Sally's Beach offers a quiet and peaceful spot for visitors looking for a private escape. Its small, intimate size adds to the charm, while soft sands and gentle waves make it a wonderful spot for wading and picnicking. The beach has picnic areas and basic facilities, providing a simple yet memorable seaside experience.

Little Harbor Beach - Little Harbor Beach is a secluded, lesser-known beach that offers a sense of discovery. Flanked by grassy dunes, it offers a quiet escape from the crowds. Its calm, clear waters make it a prime location for swimming, snorkeling, and paddleboarding. Visitors can wander along the soft sands while scanning for sea glass and small shells.

Souris Sand Spit - Souris Sand Spit is a scenic beach formation extending into the sea, offering stunning views of the coastline. Its narrow strip of sand provides a great place for a peaceful stroll or a quiet day of relaxation. Visitors can enjoy views of the town of Souris and watch ferries as they depart for Île's de la Madeleine.

Wood Islands Beach - Located near the Wood Islands Ferry Terminal, this beach is known for its red sandstone cliffs, soft sands, and iconic lighthouse. It's a great spot to watch ferries come and go or to enjoy a picnic along the shore. Visitors can explore the lighthouse and learn about PEI's maritime history.

Pinette Beach - Pinette Beach offers a calm, shallow bay with warm calm waters, making it an ideal spot for families. Surrounded by lush, natural greenery, this quiet beach is great for walking, swimming, and beachcombing.

Common Artifacts Found on the Points East Coastal Drive:

1. **Driftwood**: Points East is one of the best places to find driftwood. Beaches like Greenwich, Panmure Island, and Bothwell Beach are known for their large, sculptural driftwood pieces.
2. **Sea Glass**: Basin Head and Souris Beach are prime locations for sea glass collecting, with frosted pieces of green, white, and sometimes rare cobalt blue glass.
3. **Shells**: Collectors will find an abundance of razor clams, cockles, whelk shells, and smaller shells washed ashore, especially after storms.
4. **Fossils**: Beaches like Bothwell and Greenwich occasionally reveal small fossils embedded in the sandstone.
5. **Red Sandstone Rocks and Pebbles**: The erosion of red cliffs along beaches like Basin Head leaves smooth pebbles, great for pocket keepsakes or decor.
6. **Pottery Shards and Historical Artifacts**: Given the historic fishing communities along the Points East Coastal Drive, there is potential to find small shards of pottery, especially at Souris Beach and Panmure Island.

7. **Shipwreck Artifacts**: Shipwreck debris is rare but not unheard of. After storms, visitors sometimes spot old wooden planks and nails that may be remnants of lost vessels.

8. **Fishing and Maritime Relics**: Fishing villages like North Lake and Souris make it more common to find lobster trap tags, rope, and the occasional buoy.

9. **Bottles and Coins**: Old bottles and coins sometimes wash up along Panmure Island Beach and Basin Head. Searching after high tide or a storm increases your chances of finding these items.

Chapter 5

Special Features: Island Beach Culture And Festivals By Coastal Drive

PEI's beach culture is as rich and diverse as its coastline, with each coastal drive offering a unique blend of history, tradition, and lively festivities. From the laid-back fishing villages of the North Cape Coastal Drive to the artsy enclaves along the Central Coastal Drive and the serene, nature-filled Points East Coastal Drive, the island's beach culture is a reflection of its maritime heritage and deep connection to the sea. In this chapter, we explore the distinctive beach culture and vibrant festivals found along each of PEI's well-known coastal drives.

North Cape Coastal Drive - The North Cape Coastal Drive is known for its strong maritime identity, small fishing villages, and rugged coastal beauty. The beach culture here is steeped in local folklore, fishing traditions, and a slower, more reflective pace of life. Here's what makes this coastal drive's beach experience so memorable:

Beach Culture

· **Maritime Heritage:** Fishing is at the heart of North Cape's beach life. Villages like Tignish, Skinners Pond, and Alberton offer a glimpse into the lives of PEI's fishers, many of whom still rely on lobster, mussels, and Irish moss harvesting as a livelihood. Visitors often see brightly colored fishing boats bobbing in the harbors or unloading the day's catch.

Festivals and Events

· **Stompin' Tom Festival:** Celebrating the life and music of one of PEI's most beloved cultural icons, this festival is held in Skinners Pond, where Stompin' Tom Connors' childhood home is now a museum and cultural center. The festival features live music, storytelling, and local food.

· **Seaweed Festival:** Miminegash's connection to Irish moss harvesting is celebrated annually with the Seaweed Festival. Attendees learn about the Irish moss industry, enjoy seaweed-based foods, and experience hands-on activities like moss harvesting and cooking demos.

· **PEI International Shellfish Festival (Province-wide):** While the main festivities occur in Charlottetown, the North Cape Coastal Drive region offers its own unique shellfish-related attractions. Notably, the PEI Shellfish Museum in Tyne Valley provides an in-depth look into the history and significance of the local shellfish industry. Visitors can explore interactive displays, aquariums, and touch tanks, gaining insights into oyster cultivation and the broader shellfish culture of the area. Local restaurants along the Central Coastal Drive often offer "Shellfish Specials," and festival-themed food experiences abound.

· **North Cape Wind Energy Festival:** North Cape is also home to PEI's wind farm, and this festival highlights the island's commitment to renewable energy. Visitors can learn about wind energy while enjoying food, music, and interactive family-friendly activities.

Central Coastal Drive -Central Coastal Drive is the heart of PEI's tourism industry, known for its famous attractions, Anne of Green Gables heritage, and its family friendly beaches. This is where beach culture thrives in a lively, bustling environment filled with music, food, and family fun.

Beach Culture

- **Active Adventures:** Rustico Beach, Stanhope Beach, and Brackley Beach are popular for water sports like kayaking, paddleboarding, and snorkeling. These beaches offer easy access to rental equipment, making it simple for tourists to try something new.
- **Anne of Green Gables Connection:** The beach culture here is intertwined with Anne's literary legacy. Green Gables Heritage Place is nearby, and visitors can experience Anne-inspired picnics, dress-up activities, and storytelling sessions.

Festivals and Events

- **Cavendish Beach Music Festival:** The Cavendish Beach Music Festival is PEI's largest music event, attracting thousands of visitors each July. Major international artists headline the festival, which takes place on the grounds near Cavendish Beach. It's a must-attend event for country music fans.
- **PEI International Shellfish Festival (Province-wide):** While it's officially based in Charlottetown, this festival's influence extends to Central Coastal communities. Local restaurants along the Central Coastal Drive often offer "Shellfish Specials," and festival-themed

food experiences abound.

- **Rustico Day:** Rustico Beach comes alive during Rustico Day, a community celebration featuring a parade, local seafood, games for kids, and live music. It's a celebration of the town's Acadian roots and maritime heritage.
- **Cultural Heritage Days:** Central Coastal villages like Victoria-by-the-Sea and New London host "Cultural Heritage Days," where visitors can learn about the area's shipbuilding history, watch artisan demonstrations, and enjoy music and food.

Points East Coastal Drive - The Points East Coastal Drive is a haven for nature lovers, artists, and those seeking serenity. Beach culture here revolves around unspoiled nature, lighthouses, and a love for exploring the island's diverse shoreline.

Beach Culture

- **Natural Beauty and Conservation:** Beaches like Basin Head, Greenwich, and Panmure Island are treasured for their natural beauty. Many of these beaches are part of protected areas or national parks, which help maintain their pristine condition. This drive has beaches famous for their "singing sands" and the floating boardwalks of Greenwich.
- **Lighthouse Legacy:** Points East is home to several iconic lighthouses that offer sweeping views of the coastline. Lighthouses like Panmure Island Lighthouse and East Point Lighthouse are cultural landmarks where visitors can tour and learn about the island's maritime history.
- **Artisan Craft and Beach Artifacts:** The abundance of sea glass, driftwood, and shells has inspired local artisans to create one-of-a-kind jewelry, sculptures, and art pieces. Markets and craft fairs along Points East Coastal Drive showcase these unique, handmade

creations.

Festivals and Events

- **Basin Head Day:** This festival celebrates the unique "singing sands" of Basin Head Beach. With music, sandcastle competitions, and local food vendors, this family-friendly event highlights one of PEI's most iconic beaches.
- **PEI Shellfish Festival (Province-wide):** While the Shellfish Festival is based in Charlottetown, its influence extends across the island - especially in Points East, where oysters, mussels, and clams are harvested. Some Points East communities host mini shellfish events or offer "oyster shucking" lessons.
- **Lighthouse Tours and Celebrations:** Many Points East lighthouses host seasonal events or "Lighthouse Days" where visitors can enjoy guided tours, special exhibits, and interactive activities for kids.

Conclusion - Each of PEI's coastal drives has a unique beach culture that reflects its history, geography, and community spirit. From the quiet reflection and maritime heritage of the North Cape Coastal Drive to the lively, family-oriented Central Coastal Drive and finally to the art, nature, and serenity of the Points East Coastal Drive, PEI's beach culture is as diverse as its landscapes. Festivals and events bring these coastal communities together, offering locals and tourists the chance to celebrate music, seafood, art, and maritime history. No matter which coastal drive you choose to explore, you'll find the heart and soul of PEI's beach life waiting to be discovered.

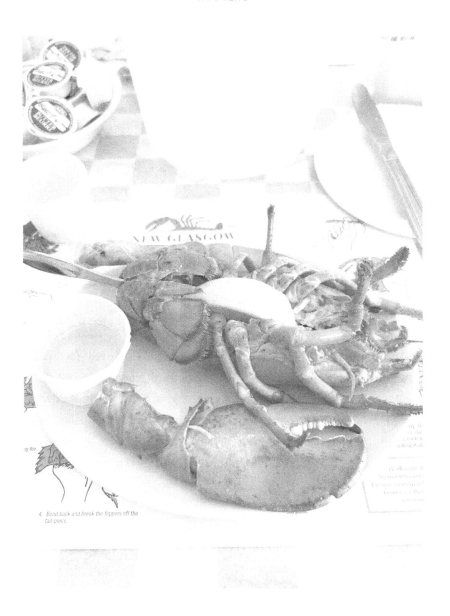

4. Bend back and break the flippers off the tail-piece.

Chapter 6

Extra: Cruise to Île de la Madeleine From Souris For More Exquisite Beaches

Imagine embarking on a scenic cruise across the Gulf of St. Lawrence, with the promise of adventure, culture, and the discovery of some of the most pristine beaches in Canada. A cruise from Souris, Prince Edward Island, to Île de la Madeleine (Magdalen Islands) offers exactly that. With picturesque views of the open sea and a chance to explore the exquisite beaches of Île de la Madeleine, this unique journey is a perfect addition to any PEI beach adventure.

The Cruise Experience
   Departure Point: Souris, PEI (Ferry Terminal)
   Destination: Île de la Madeleine, Quebec
   Duration: Approximately 5 hours
   Ferry Operator: CTMA Ferry (Cooperative de Transport Maritime et Aérien)

Travelers can board the CTMA ferry at the Souris ferry terminal, which is conveniently located along PEI's Points East Coastal Drive. This ferry provides a comfortable, scenic voyage across the Gulf of St. Lawrence. As you sail, you'll witness breathtaking views of the endless ocean, occasional seabird sightings, and perhaps even a glimpse of a whale or two.

Onboard Amenities:

- Dining options with fresh seafood and local cuisine
- Lounge areas with panoramic ocean views
- Entertainment for children and families
- Restrooms and changing facilities
- Options for vehicle transport, so you can bring your car along for island exploration

The CTMA ferry operates year-round, but peak travel season is in the summer months, from June to September. Booking tickets in advance is highly recommended, especially if you plan to bring a vehicle.

Exploring Île de la Madeleine - Once you disembark at Île de la Madeleine, you'll be greeted by a stunning island landscape defined by rugged red cliffs, golden sandy beaches, and quaint seaside villages. The island is part of the province of Quebec, but its unique Acadian culture and maritime charm make it feel like its own world.

Here's a guide to the island's beaches, activities, and local culture.

Top Beaches to Explore

Dune du Sud - This famous beach is known for its dramatic red sandstone cliffs and long, golden shorelines. Small caves and natural rock formations make it one of the island's most scenic beachscapes. It's a popular spot for beachcombing, sunbathing, and exploring natural caves.

Plage de la Grande Échouerie (Old Harry Beach) - One of the island's most beloved beaches, Old Harry Beach boasts soft white sand, crystal-clear waters, and rolling dunes. It's a prime location for swimming, kayaking, and leisurely walks along the shore.

Plage de la Pointe-aux-Loups - This expansive beach connects two of the smaller islands in the archipelago. Its calm waters make it a family-friendly spot for swimming and water activities. The area's natural beauty and soft sand are ideal for sunbathing and beach picnics.

Plage de l'Ouest - This beach faces the open ocean and is known for its wilder, windier conditions, making it a top spot for surfing and kitesurfing. The rugged beauty of this beach is unmatched, and it's often less crowded than other beaches on the island.

Plage de la Martinique - This long, sandy beach is popular for family outings and leisurely swims. With calm waters and a relaxed vibe, it's a perfect spot for kids to splash and play.

Adventures and Activities on Île de la Madeleine - Île de la Madeleine offers more than just sun and sand. Adventure seekers, nature enthusiasts, and cultural travelers will all find something to love. Here are some top activities to try during your visit.

1. Water Sports and Outdoor Activities

- **Kayaking and Paddleboarding**: Paddle along the calm waters surrounding the islands, with guided tours often available.

- **Surfing and Kitesurfing**: The island's west-facing beaches have strong winds and surf-perfect conditions for kitesurfers and surfers.
- **Snorkeling and Diving**: Discover underwater life in the clear waters around the island.

2. Cultural Experiences

- **Traditional Music and Acadian Heritage**: Experience live music performances, storytelling, and dance at local cultural centers.
- **Fishing Excursions**: Join a lobster or mussel fishing tour with local fishers and experience an authentic maritime adventure.
- **Artisan Markets**: Local artisans craft unique jewelry, pottery, and handmade souvenirs inspired by the island's natural surroundings.

3. Nature and Wildlife Tours

- **Whale Watching**: Join a guided boat tour to spot whales, seals, and other marine life in the surrounding waters.
- **Birdwatching**: The island's cliffs and wetlands attract a variety of seabirds, including puffins, gannets, and terns.
- **Hiking and Coastal Walks**: Explore the island's coastal trails, which offer panoramic views of cliffs, sea stacks, and open waters.

Practical Tips for Visiting Île de la Madeleine

- **Book the Ferry Early**: The CTMA ferry is a popular option for visitors, so booking your ticket in advance (especially during summer) is essential.
- **Pack for Adventure**: Bring comfortable walking shoes, swimwear, and weather-appropriate clothing, as island weather can change

rapidly.

- **Plan for Island Time**: Life on Île de la Madeleine is slower paced, so embrace the relaxed vibe and plan to take your time exploring.
- **Currency and Language**: The island is part of Quebec, so French is the dominant language, but many locals speak English. Canadian dollars are used throughout.

Conclusion - A cruise from Souris, PEI, to Île de la Madeleine is an unforgettable journey that adds an adventurous chapter to any PEI beach vacation. From the ferry's scenic views to the island's stunning beaches, charming inns, and thrilling outdoor activities, Île de la Madeleine offers a vibrant blend of natural beauty, culture, and adventure. Whether you're relaxing on Dune du Sud's golden sands or kitesurfing along Plage de l'Ouest, every moment is a new discovery. For those seeking an island-hopping experience, this cruise is a must-do addition to your PEI beach journey.

Resources

Beaches & Parks | Tourism PEI. (n.d.).
https://www.tourismpei.com/what-to-do/beaches-parks
Welcome PEI. (2024, August 22). *Home - Welcome PEI.*
https://welcomepei.com/
The Beach Guide & Copyright - The World Beach Guide. (2023, August 29). *The 10 best beaches in Prince Edward Island.*
https://www.worldbeachguide.com/canada/prince-edward-island
Gemma. (2023, September 14). *19+ of the best beaches in PEI, Canada.* Off Track Travel. https://offtracktravel.ca/best-beaches-pei-canada/
The best beaches in PEI. (n.d.). Destination Canada. https://travel.destin ationcanada.com/en-us/things-to-do/best-beaches-pei
Scott, K. (2018, January 15). Beachcombing in Prince Edward Island, Canada. *Beachcombing Magazine.* https://www.beachcombingmagazi ne.com/blogs/news/destination-beach-glass-prince-edward-island-canada
Artefacts of Prince Edward Island Community Museums. (n.d.). Artefacts of Prince Edward Island Community Museums.
https://artefactspei.weebly.com/
Homepage | Tourisme Îles de la Madeleine. (n.d.).
https://www.tourismeilesdelamadeleine.com/en/?gad_source=1&gcl id=CjwKCAiAyJS7BhBiEiwAyS9uNb9wFa799Iwk_t60E-FhTp2T0bGT mPYWyW1v9nZGaCBjMW4eavx5sB0C-m4QAvD_BwE

User, S. (2024, December 17). *Home - CTMA.*
https://www.traversierctma.ca/en/

The pictures in the printed book are in black and white, the pictures in the e-book are in color!

If you find all the details and vivid descriptions in this book helpful and engaging, I would be very appreciative if you left a favorable review for the book on Amazon!

Made in United States
Cleveland, OH
28 March 2025

15598562R00030